HIDE & SEEK

Written by Diana Noonan
Photographs by Audrie Leslie

What's this?

A nut?

Or a spider?

Some creatures
pretend,
and others hide.

This tiny caterpillar
has “eye” patterns
on its skin.

It’s pretending to be
a dangerous snake
so that other creatures
will keep away.

These moths are
hiding from birds.

Can you find
the moth
in each photo?

What's this?
A twig?
Or a moth?

These special moths hide all day and come out at night when the hungry birds have gone to sleep.

This spider is pretending to be a twig, too.

A caterpillar hides its cocoon behind leaves.

Sea anemones hide under shells and sand,

but when it's time for dinner...

they soon come out!

No one would ever guess this pile of seaweed...

is a crab.

Next time you're out walking,
try playing animal hide and seek.
You never know what you might find.